When Tilly Turtle came to tea,
She took a taxi to the tree,
Where the party was to be,
When Tilly Turtle came to tea.

When Tilly Turtle came to tea,
She arrived on time at three,

Looking pretty as could be,
When Tilly Turtle came to tea.

When Tilly Turtle came to tea,
There were tiny teacups set for three,

And toast and tarts beneath the tree,
When Tilly Turtle came to tea.

When Tilly Turtle came to tea,
Her friends Tiger and Toad and she,
Told tall tales and laughed with glee,
When Tilly Turtle came to tea.

When Tilly Turtle came to tea,
She laughed so hard she could not see,
And tipped the table with her knee,
When Tilly Turtle came to tea.

When Tilly Turtle came to tea,
The teacups tumbled, oh dear me!

What a terrible sight to see!
When Tilly Turtle came to tea.

When Tilly Turtle came to tea,
She told her friends, "Please pardon me,
For the topsy-turvy mess you see!"
When Tilly Turtle came to tea.

When Tilly Turtle came to tea,
She said, "If you will both agree,
Please put the tablecloth on me!"
When Tilly Turtle came to tea.

When Tilly Turtle came to tea,
She saved the party cheerfully.

She turned into a table—see?
When Tilly Turtle came to tea.

How many things can you find that begin with the letter T?

See inside back cover for answers.

Tt Cheer

T is for turtle, tiger, and toad
T is for taxi driving down the road
T is for table and telephone booth
T is for teacup, tickle, and tooth
Hooray for T, big and small—
the most totally terrific letter of all!